Full-Speed Sports

The Science of a Carve Turn

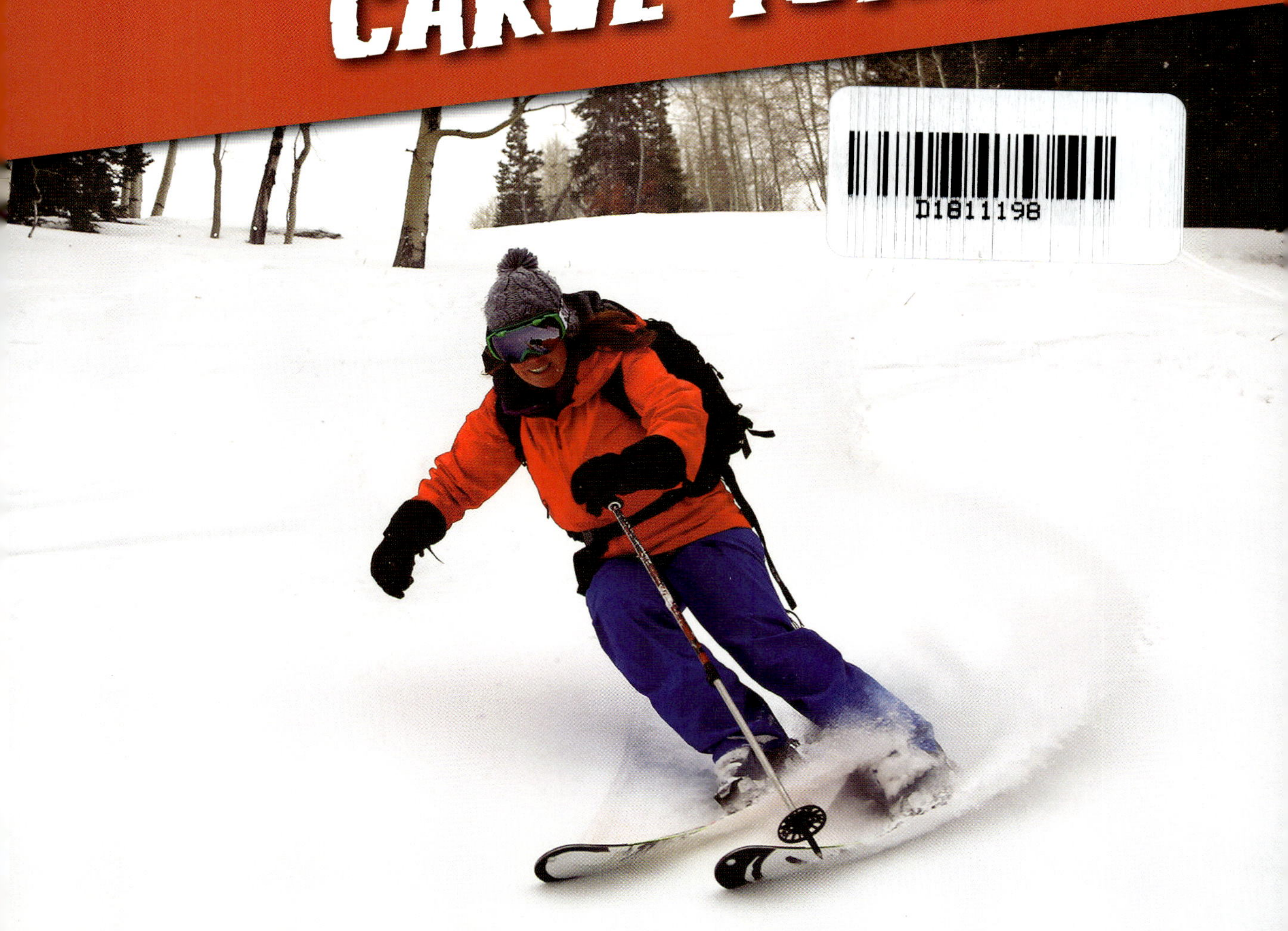

Nel Yomtov

Published in the United States of America by Cherry Lake Publishing
Ann Arbor, Michigan
www.cherrylakepublishing.com

Content Adviser: Dr. John Eric Goff, Professor of Physics and Chair of the Physics Department
at Lynchburg College, and author of *Gold Medal Physics*
Reading Advisor: Marla Conn, ReadAbility, Inc.

Photo Credits: ©Johnny Adolphson/Shutterstock.com, cover, 1; ©Mitch Gunn/Shutterstock.com, 5, 13, 16;
©B.Stefanov/Shutterstock.com, 6; ©technotr /iStock.com, 9; ©Design Pics/Newscom, 10; ©Alex Egorov/
Shutterstock.com, 15; ©Jupiterimages/Thinkstock, 19; ©Denis Pepin/Shutterstock.com, 20;
©usas/iStock.com, 22; ©INTERFOTO/Alamy, 25; ©PCN Photography/Alamy, 26

Library of Congress Cataloging-in-Publication Data

Yomtov, Nelson.
  The science of a carve turn/Nel Yomtov.
     pages cm.—(Full-Speed Sports)
  Includes index.
  Audience: Age: 8–12.
  Audience: Grade: 4 to 6.
  ISBN 978-1-63362-580-8 (hardcover)—ISBN 978-1-63362-760-4 (pdf)—ISBN 978-1-63362-670-6 (paperback)—
ISBN 978-1-63362-850-2 (ebook)
  1. Skis and skiing—Juvenile literature. I. Title.

  GV854.315.Y66 2015
  796.93—dc23

                         2014049843

Cherry Lake Publishing would like to acknowledge the work of
the Partnership for 21st Century Skills. Please visit *www.p21.org*
for more information.

Printed in the United States of America
Corporate Graphics

ABOUT THE AUTHOR

Nel Yomtov is an award-winning author of nonfiction books and graphic novels for young readers.
He lives in the New York City area.

TABLE OF CONTENTS

CHAPTER 1

THE RACE IS ON!

Gina and her brother, Ron, were watching an Olympic skiing event on television. As the skier positioned himself at the top of the huge, snow-covered slope, Gina asked, "What did you say the name of this event is?"

"It's called **slalom**," Ron said. "The goal of the skier is to pass between a series of poles, called gates, as fast as he can, without missing any."

"Then other skiers take their turns. The winner has the fastest combined time from two runs down the slope, right?" Gina asked.

"Right," Ron replied. "Look! The skier is about to take off!"

"Wow, look how fast he's going!" Gina said.

The skier sped down the slope, sharply weaving in and out of the gates. He used the poles he held in each hand to balance and **propel** himself down the slope. Each time he passed a gate, his skis kicked up a huge plume of powdery snow.

Marsel Hirscher performs a carve turn in a slalom race in Bulgaria in 2012.

Šárka Záhrobská skis in a race in France in 2010.

"He looks like he's going to fall over each time he makes one of those quick, short turns," Gina said. "How can he go so fast and turn so sharply and not fall down?"

"He does it by making a special kind of turn called a **carve**," Ron said. "It allows him to keep moving down the mountain without losing much speed."

"It looks like a tricky move," Gina said. "Can you teach me how to carve the next time we go skiing?"

"I can try!" Ron promised.

Downhill skiing is lots of fun. But racers have to make exact, split-second decisions and body movements, sometimes while traveling at speeds up to 100 miles (161 kilometers) per hour. Ski equipment—clothing, boots, skis, poles, and helmet—is heavy and makes a run down the slope even more demanding. Physical forces, such as **gravity** and **friction**, act upon the skier.

None of these challenges, however, are new to the sport of skiing. Skiers have been facing these issues for thousands of years.

GO DEEPER!

Reread this chapter about downhill skiing and carving. What is the main idea? What challenges does a competitive skier face? Are any physical forces involved in skiing? If so, name a few.

CHAPTER 2

A Look at the Past

The origin of skiing dates back to about 6000 BCE. More than 200 prehistoric man-made skis have been uncovered, mainly in Russia and the Scandinavian countries of Norway, Sweden, and Finland. The oldest ski was found in Russia and is about 8,300 years old. Archaeologists have also discovered ancient paintings and rock carvings that show people on skis.

Norse **mythology** and legends feature many stories of skiing. The god Ull, famous for his hunting and combat skills, is known as the god of skiing. The finest

*Wooden skis, similar to these from the 1950s,
have been around for hundreds of years.*

skier in Norse folklore, however, is the goddess Skade.
Tales often describe her traveling on skis to hunt wild
animals with a bow and arrow.

Skis were an important method of transportation in
the snow-covered regions of Scandinavia. High
mountains and broad stretches of flatlands made
wintertime travel difficult. Crossing snowy **terrain** on
skis enabled people to maintain contact with each other
and played a vital role in hunting and trapping. Early skis
were made of different types of wood and sometimes

Hundreds of years ago, people used skis to help them hunt wild animals.

LOOK!

Look at this drawing carefully. How could skiing help ancient people hunt? What other activities do you think ancient people performed on skis? Go online to find out more.

covered with animal hide or fabric. People used different shapes and sizes of skis on different types of terrain and snow conditions.

By the 1700s, skis were also being used in warfare. Accounts of the Scanian War (1675–1679), fought mainly between Denmark-Norway and the Swedish Empire, tell of soldiers carrying muskets and skiing up to 60 miles (96.5 km) a day. In 1716, troops from Russia, Sweden, and Norway waged battles in the Great Northern War entirely on skis.

In the mid-1800s, people began skiing for recreation instead of warfare. Norwegians used the beautiful countryside of the Lyngen Alps to ski. They established ski clubs, ski lodges, and skiing competitions for people of all economic classes. Ski racing became popular. By this time, skiing was catching on in many parts of the world. In the United States, the first known use of recreational skis was in Wisconsin in 1841.

Downhill ski racing emerged in Norway by the 1860s and quickly spread. In 1922, Sir Arnold Lunn, an Englishman, developed the first modern slalom by introducing the slalom gates—the pair of poles between which the skier must pass. In 1924, the first international slalom competition was held in Mürren, Switzerland. Downhill skiing became an Olympic event at the 1936 Winter Olympic Games held in Garmisch-Partenkirchen, Germany.

As skiing evolved, so did the skis themselves. The earliest skis were made of wood. Simple straps made of leather or tree roots were used to bind the ski to the foot. In the mid-20th century, manufacturers began to use new materials such as plywood, aluminum, fiberglass, and plastic.

Today, skis are available in many different materials, sizes, and shapes. These modern improvements provide skiers with the best tools to achieve one of the sport's greatest sensations—the carve.

Marlies Schild's equipment helped her ski quickly and smoothly.

CHAPTER 3

THE CARVE

Many physical forces act upon a skier while speeding down the slope. Gravity pulls the skier down the slope. Friction, which slows down the skier, is created between the bottom of the skis and the surface of the slope. Aerodynamic **drag** acts on the skier as she moves through the surrounding air.

With such forces at work, how does a skier make sharp, tight, and *controlled* turns through each gate? Most experts agree that the most effective way is to make carve turns.

By cutting the edge of his skis into the snow, the skier can turn more quickly.

In a carve turn, the goal of the skier is to cut the edges of his skis deeply enough into the snow so that the skis do not skid sideways, away from his body. Skidding slows down the skier by creating more friction between the ski and the snow. As the skier carves, the skis travel along their length in the curved arc cut into the snow and take the skier around in a turn.

Slalom skiers generally use carving skis. Unlike straight, rectangular skis, carving skis are thinner in the middle and have wider, curved front and back ends.

Chemmy Alcott crouches down to reduce drag.

Therefore, the side edges of the skis curve inward and back out again. To begin the turn, the skier leans, or rolls, both knees to one side. As he does, the edges of the skis bend into the snow, creating a curved path. The more the knees are leaned over, the more the ski will bend, and the tighter and sharper the curve will be.

To start a new turn, a skier shifts his body until the bottom of the skis are flat against the snow and his body is **perpendicular** to the slope. Then he rolls his knees to the direction opposite the one of the first turn and begins to cut into the snow with the edges of his skis again.

A perfectly carved turn eliminates almost all skidding. With snow and friction minimized, the skier keeps greater control. In fact, some experts claim that a skier who carves properly will go almost as fast as if he or she had skied straight down the slope!

A skier further maximizes his speed by reducing aerodynamic drag. He does this by skiing in a crouch position. This minimizes the surface area of the front of his body. The less frontal area, the less air resistance. The result is greater speed.

THINK ABOUT IT!

Describe how gravity and friction act upon a downhill skier. When skiing downhill, is less friction better? Why? How can a skier use friction to slow down or stop? If a skier were having trouble performing his or her carve turn, what advice would you give? Reread this chapter for some ideas.

CHAPTER 4

DANGER ON THE SLOPES?

The ski equipment manufacturer Elan introduced carving skis in the early 1990s. Within a decade, they had become a favorite for people at all ability levels, from the beginner to the professional competitive skier. There are many advantages of the carving ski. Because it is typically shorter and lighter than a traditional ski, it offers greater **maneuverability**. The wider front and back allow for easier turning. Many beginners claim these features help them learn skiing faster. People also report that the skis are so easy to turn that skiing is less tiring. Carving skis also offer a better grip on icy surfaces and do not skid sideways as much as traditional skis.

Carving and the carving ski, however, also present dangers that all skiers must consider. Most important, when carving, the skier goes faster—which in certain

It's common for skiers to fall while practicing carve turns.

At a ski resort, like this one in Quebec, skiers need to be aware of one another.

circumstances can be very dangerous. Keep in mind that carving is not only performed in competitive slalom racing. Many skiers use the technique while on the slopes for fun. Coming out of a carve turn at high speed can present a danger to the skier and to others on the slopes.

In *Carving: Fascination on Skis*, Johannes Roschinsky writes, "Because of the special characteristics of the carving ski, some skiers, drawing on their skiing ability, overdo things and try to carve down the whole breadth of the slope at too high a speed. Such people not only endanger themselves, they also endanger many, mostly slower, skiers."

Some studies indicate that carving skis do not significantly increase the risk of injury to the user. Other studies report the risk of experiencing ACL injuries in recreational downhill skiing is actually reduced by the use of carving skis. The ACL is one of the four major **ligaments** of the human knee. Most experts, however, agree that additional research in this field is needed.

GO DEEPER!

Think about what you've read in this chapter. What are the advantages of carving and a carving ski? What are the potential dangers of carving? What types of injuries do you think are most common among skiers? Name a few strategies to help avoid skiing injuries.

Falling uphill into the snow is safer than falling forwards.

[21ST CENTURY SKILLS LIBRARY]

Whether you carve or not, there are many ways to get hurt on the slopes. Here are a few tips on how to avoid injury:

- Stay in shape. Stretch regularly and get plenty of exercise year-round.
- Start out slow. Ski on easy hills (marked as green circles) to learn new movements or warm up before moving on to more difficult slopes (blue squares and black diamonds).
- Be considerate of others on the slopes. Give yourself plenty of room to stop or dodge others. Give downhill skiers the right of way.
- Take breaks between runs and drink plenty of liquids.
- Let yourself fall. If you start to fall backward, it's better to simply sit down than try to stay standing. Resisting a fall with jerky movements of the body can result in serious injury.
- Take lessons. Learn the proper techniques from a professional ski instructor.

CHAPTER 5

Kings and Queens of the Slopes

Many outstanding athletes have gained international fame and fortune in competitive slalom skiing. These skiers have mastered the carve turn and other fundamentals of ski racing.

Alberto Tomba was born near Bologna, Italy, in 1966. When he was younger, he participated in tennis, soccer, and dirt bike racing, but found his true calling in skiing. On November 27, 1987, he captured his first Alpine Ski World Cup victory in the slalom. Two days later, he won the giant slalom—a longer course than the slalom, with wider gates that are set farther apart. In 1988, Tomba won gold medals at the Winter Olympic Games in slalom and giant slalom. At the Winter Games in 1992, he won gold in the giant slalom and also captured the silver medal in the slalom. At his third Olympics in 1994, he again took home the

Alberto Tomba is a slalom champion.

Phil Mahre broke his leg while practicing for the 1980 Lake Placid Olympics.

silver medal in the slalom, giving him a total of five Olympic medals. Tomba's flashy style, on and off the slopes, made him an idol in Italy, where he was nicknamed "Tomba La Bomba."

Many experts consider Phil Mahre the best technical ski racer the United States has ever produced. He was born in Washington State in 1957. In 1979, he severely fractured his **tibia** at the pre-Olympic races at Lake Placid. The injury required surgery and several screws

THINK ABOUT IT!

A debate between people who use "planks" (skis) and those who prefer "trays" (snowboards) has been going on for years. Compare the two sports. How do the body and feet positions of each sport differ? Which sport do you think is easier to learn? Why? Which sport is more convenient to participate in? Which sport is more dangerous? Why?

and a metal plate in his ankle to hold the bones together. But Mahre made an astonishing recovery and won the silver medal in the slalom the following year. Mahre capped off his incredible comeback by capturing the gold medal in the slalom at the 1984 Winter Olympics.

Mikaela Shiffrin, born in Colorado, is the youngest slalom champion in Olympic skiing history, at 18 years and 345 days. She was favored to win the event at the 2014 Winter Olympics in Sochi, Russia, and led all of her competitors after the first run. She nearly fell in her second run, but held on to win, beating second-place Marlies Schild of Austria. Shiffrin opened the 2015 racing season with a bang, competing in her first World Cup championship. She tied for first place in the giant slalom event.

TIMELINE

A TIMELINE HISTORY OF SKIING

Prehistory	Hunters and trappers use flat, wooden skis, often covered with horsehide, and a single pole for balance.
1716	War between Russia, Sweden, and Norway is fought mainly on skis.
Mid-1800s	Norwegians begin skiing the Lyngen Alps for recreation instead of warfare. Narrow skis are designed for quick gliding on racing trails.
1870	The first modern hourglass-shaped ski is introduced. This narrow ski flexes easily on the snow, ideal for smooth carving and turning.
1949	Aluminum skis become widespread.
Early 1960s	Skis made of fiberglass begin to replace aluminum skis.
1982	The Canadian Ski Hall of Fame opens.
Early 1990s	Carving skis, with much wider front and back ends, become popular. They bend into a shape and help the carved turn.
2000s	Rocker skis—a bow-shaped design that sharply curves upward at both ends—are introduced. Modern ski materials include wood (birch, maple, fir, ash, and others), carbon, Kevlar (a material used in bulletproof vests), various plastics, fiberglass, and titanium.
2004	Filmmaker Warren Miller releases his 55th, and last, ski documentary movie (having made one every year since 1950).
2014	The Winter Olympics, in Sochi, Russia, feature women's ski jumping for the first time.

THINK ABOUT IT

How has skiing changed over the years? What were the early uses of skis? What materials are modern skis made of?

Reread chapter 3. What physical forces act upon a downhill skier? Describe how a carve turn is made.

Watch a slalom race on television or the Internet, and carefully observe what the skier does from the top of the slope to the bottom.

Describe the sequence of the skier's movements while racing downhill and passing through the gates.

LEARN MORE

FURTHER READING

Barr, George. *Sports Science for Young People*. New York: Dover Publications, 2011.

Burns, Kylie. *Alpine and Freestyle Skiing*. New York: Crabtree Publishing Company, 2010.

Deutsch, Jessica. *Downhill Skiing for Fun!* Minneapolis: Compass Point Books, 2009.

WEB SITES

How Stuff Works—How Snow Skis Work
http://adventure.howstuffworks.com/outdoor-activities/snow-sports/snow-skis.htm
Get the inside scoop on the latest developments in snow ski materials and design, and how they have impacted the world of skiing.

National Geographic—Ski Cross
http://education.nationalgeographic.com/education/media/skiing/?ar_a=1Fact
Learn about the history of skiing from the Stone Age to the present, and check out audio and video clips about different skiing techniques.

Science Kids—The Physics of Skiing
www.sciencekids.co.nz/videos/sports/skiing.html
Watch an exciting video to learn how acceleration, gravity, friction, and other forces of nature relate to downhill skiing.

GLOSSARY

carve (CARVE) a type of turn in which the skier creates a path by forcing the edge of the skis into the snow so that the ski travels along the path in a circular movement

drag (DRAG) a force which slows down the movement of an object

friction (FRIK-shuhn) the force that resists motion between two objects and slows them down

gravity (GRAV-i-tee) the force that pulls objects toward the center of the earth

ligaments (LIG-uh-muhnts) tough bands of tissue that connect bones

maneuverability (muh-noo-vur-uh-BIL-i-tee) the quality of being easy to move, especially in situations that need care or skill

mythology (mi-THAH-luh-jee) a group of old stories and tales that express the beliefs or history of a particular culture or religion

perpendicular (pur-puhn-DIK-yuh-lur) positioned at a right angle, 90 degrees to another surface straight up and down

propel (pruh-PEL) to push an object forward

slalom (SLAH-luhm) an athletic event in which competitors ski down a hill, zigzagging between a series of gates

terrain (tuh-RAYN) the surface features of an area of land

tibia (TIB-ee-uh) the shinbone, which connects the knee to the ankle

INDEX